POULTRY

FARM TO MARKET

Jason Cooper

Rourke Publications, Inc.
Vero Beach, Florida 32964

Edited by Pamela J.P. Schroeder

PHOTO CREDITS
All photos © Lynn M. Stone

Library of Congress Cataloging-in-Publication Data
Cooper, Jason, 1942-
    Poultry / by Jason Cooper.
       p. cm. — (Farm to market)
    Summary: Describes where and how North American poultry is
raised, what poultry products are, and how they are processed
and marketed.
    ISBN 0-86625-618-0
    1. Poultry—Juvenile literature. 2. Poultry products—Juvenile
literature. 3. Poultry—North America—Juvenile literature.
4. Poultry products—North America—Juvenile literature.
[1. Poultry.] I. Title. II. Series: Cooper, Jason, 1942-
Farm to market.
SF487.5.C66 1997
636.5—dc21   97-13233
                             CIP
                             AC

Printed in the USA

TABLE OF CONTENTS

POULTRY

Birds that farmers raise for their meat or eggs are called poultry. The most popular kinds of poultry in North America are chickens and turkeys. Between the two, chickens are by far the more common birds.

Not every country shares North America's love of chicken and turkey meat. Birds called guinea fowl, or guinea hens, are popular in France. Eastern Europeans like farm-raised, or **domestic** (duh MESS tihk), geese.

Chickens are the birds most often raised for food in North America. Some breeds are best for meat. Others are best for eggs.

KINDS OF POULTRY

In addition to chickens, turkeys, guinea fowl, and geese, domestic ducks are poultry. A few quail and pheasants are raised as poultry, too.

Chicken farmers raise many different **breeds** (BREEDZ). Each breed, or type, of chicken has its good points. Some breeds are best for meat. Others are great egg-layers.

There are far fewer breeds of ducks, geese, and turkeys. Almost all the turkeys raised for market belong to the same white-feathered breed.

Black Java chickens, used for both meat and eggs, became very rare. Commercial poultry farms want breeds that are best for one use.

WHERE POULTRY IS RAISED

Farmers raise poultry everywhere in North America. Some areas, however, raise far more birds than others.

California, for example, produces more chicken eggs than any other state. Indiana and Pennsylvania are second and third.

Arkansas, followed by Georgia and Alabama, raises the most chickens for meat.

North Carolina is the leading turkey state, followed by Minnesota and California. Long Island, New York, raises more ducks than any other place.

California is the leading producer of chicken eggs. The eggs of other kinds of poultry are rarely eaten in North America.

HOW POULTRY IS RAISED

Huge **commercial** (ke MER shul) farms raise most of the poultry that feeds North Americans. Commercial farms are in the business of raising large numbers of birds for market.

Most commercial farms buy young birds, or chicks, from **hatcheries** (HATCH er eez). The hatcheries' birds lay eggs. Once the chicks hatch, the hatcheries ship day-old chicks to the commercial poultry farms.

The farms feed the chicks a food mix. It has things such as wheat, corn, sorghum, and protein.

Fresh from a hatchery, these baby turkeys are kept indoors for several weeks. Their indoor pens are heated.

Guinea fowl are commonly raised in France, but they are unusual in North America.

Embden breed geese stand at a watering trough they share with sheep in this pasture.

READY FOR MARKET

Most chickens on commercial farms are raised indoors. Some of the farms keep over 1 million birds!

Young turkeys are kept indoors, but most farms keep older, larger turkeys outdoors in pens or fields.

Chickens raised to lay eggs for market live in long houses. Machines deliver food and water to them automatically. Their eggs are even taken automatically. Chickens begin egg-laying when they are just 21 weeks old.

These young turkeys have been moved to outdoor pens. They find shade under roofs (right) and feed in the round, metal feeders (left).

POULTRY MEAT

Farmers raise their birds until they reach a certain age and weight. Then they are ready for **slaughter** (SLAW ter), or killing, and **processing** (PRAH sess ing). Processing makes the birds ready for eating.

Meat chickens, called broilers, are slaughtered when they weigh about 4 pounds (1.8 kilograms). They are just eight weeks old, so their meat is tender.

Ducks are slaughtered at 6 pounds (2.7 kg). Most turkeys are four to five months old and 12 to 24 pounds (5.5 to 11 kg) when they are ready for slaughter.

These turkeys are about five months old. They weigh about 20 pounds (9 kg). They are ready for slaughter and market.

PROCESSING

A few poultry farms slaughter and process their own birds. Most farms ship their poultry to a processing plant. There the birds are killed, cleaned, and packaged.

A state meat inspector is always on duty. The inspector makes sure the birds are healthy and that the plant and its machines are clean.

Processing plants ship poultry products to supermarkets and food **distributors** (dih STRIHB u terz). Nine of every 10 chickens are shipped fresh. They are kept cool, but not frozen. Most whole turkeys are quick-frozen.

Removing necks of turkeys, workers move the birds along the processing line.

POULTRY PRODUCTS

The main poultry products are meat and eggs. On average each North American eats about 245 chicken eggs every year. Each also eats about 75 pounds (34 kg) of poultry meat.

Some poultry meat is processed into hot dogs, bologna, and meat sticks.

Eggs are also used in making certain medicines and paints. Poultry feathers stuff some pillows and outdoor clothing.

Fresh turkeys near the end of the processing line are cooled in ice water.

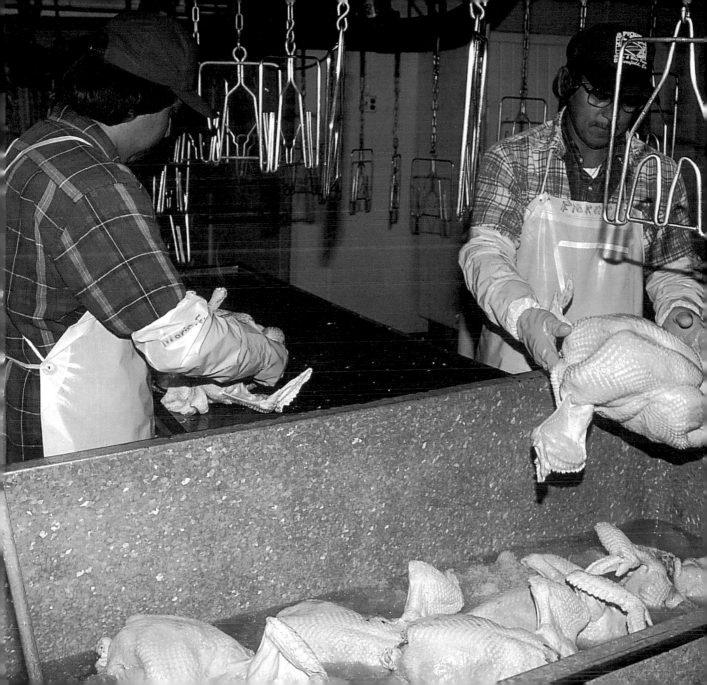

POULTRY AS FOOD

Poultry meat and eggs are a good source of protein. The human body needs protein to live and grow.

Except for the skin, poultry is a lean meat. It has little fat. Some people like poultry better than red meat because poultry has less fat.

Egg yolks have high amounts of a fatty, waxy substance called **cholesterol** (koh LES te rall). Health experts tell people to stay away from too much cholesterol. However, eggs are rich in iron, phosphorus, vitamin B-12, and minerals, all important to good health.

Glossary

breed (BREED) — a particular group or type of farm animal within a larger group of very closely related animals, such as a *barred rock* chicken among all chickens

cholesterol (koh LES te rall) — a waxy, fatty substance in human blood

commercial (ka MER shul) — something done in a big way to make money

distributor (dih STRIHB u ter) — a person or place that gathers products, such as eggs, in large numbers and re-sells them to stores

domestic (duh MESS tihk) — animals long tamed and raised by people as farm animals or pets

hatchery (HATCH er ee) — a place where eggs are hatched

processing (PRAH sess ing) — to prepare fresh fruit or meat for market

slaughter (SLAW ter) — the killing of animals for food

INDEX